God's Nudge

God's Nudge

Tekisha D. Wimbush

Copyright © 2022 J Merrill Publishing, Inc.

All rights reserved. No part of this publication may be reproduced, distributed, or transmitted in any form or by any means, including photocopying, recording, or other electronic or mechanical methods, without the prior written permission of the publisher, except in the case of brief quotations embodied in critical reviews and certain other noncommercial uses permitted by copyright law. For permission requests, write to the publisher, addressed "Attention: Permissions Coordinator," at the address below.

J Merrill Publishing, Inc.
434 Hillpine Drive
Columbus, OH 43207
www.JMerrill.pub

Library of Congress Control Number: 2021901945
ISBN-13: 978-1-950719-88-4 (Paperback)
ISBN-13: 978-1-950719-87-7 (eBook)

Book Title: God's Nudge
Author: Tekisha D. Wimbush
Editing: Dennis Brown

Contents

Acknowledgments	vii
Introduction	ix
1. Standing Strong and True	1
2. Where Do You Focus Your Attention?	5
3. What Will They Say Then?	9
4. What Will You Do To Know Peace?	13
5. The Right Heart	17
6. In Reflection, There Are Great Gains	21
7. The Mind Is A Terrible Thing To Waste	27
8. Run and Tell	31
9. Thank You, God, For The Invitation	35
10. Look Who Is At The Table	39
11. Poor and Ineffective Communication Destroys Relationships	43
12. Lord, Keep On Keeping Me	49
13. Protective Custody	53
14. Reset, Impact, Team Selection	59
15. Negativity Is Contagious	65
16. Perseverance Is An Act of Will	69
17. Rhema	73
18. We Must Persuade Them	77
19. Level Up	81
20. Know Your Worth (Part 1)	85
21. Know Your Worth (Part 2)	89
22. I Need My "Jump"	93
23. It Only Takes Two	97
24. Forever Changed	101
25. Allow The Good News That You Know About Christ To Affect Your Life	105
26. How To Declare A Thing	109
27. Loving God, Loving Others	113
28. "Hind" Strength	117

29. Active Participation, Blessed Connected	121
30. God's Grace and Mercy Makes Me Worthy	127
About the Author	131

Acknowledgments

Thank You to our Lord and Savior, Jesus Christ. God is Great and Mighty Worthy of all Praise! He is yet Methodical in all that he Does! He is Immutable and never changing.

Thank You to all the supporters of Part 1 & Part 2 of "The I Am In Me." God is not slack and is longsuffering as he desires that no soul shall perish. But that all come to repentance. It gives me great humility to present book 3, "God's Nudge," written in such a difficult time throughout our land.

Thank You to my family, friends, and loved ones.

To my husband, Bishop Willie J. Wimbush Jr., my children Jasemine, Jaden, and Jahdon, who now are all adults preparing to leave their mark on the world. My two grandchildren, Brandon and Bella, who are growing up so fast before my eyes!

My mother, Pastor Shawyl R. Williams, my Loving Church Family Church of the Reform Church of Love, Majennie Creations LLC, Focused Dreamers LLC, and the Sister 2 Sister Focus Group. They hold me accountable to the Word of God that I may study to show myself approved unto God as I develop and lead those that follow me as I follow Christ.

Finally, I thank my Granddad, Leon Jackson, who has been instrumental in my life, and all of those who have passed on that were so dear.

Introduction

Sometimes You Have To Be Reminded of Who You Are.

Have you ever been there? You needed that "Nudge."

Fear is an emotion that can be paralyzing. You needed that "Nudge" to calm your anxious thoughts, those thoughts that seem to be so real.

Unworthiness does not feel good! Especially when God Nudges you and says that in Christ, "I Am Worthy." Read God's Nudge with an open reminder of who God says you are and the invitation to get to know Him!

Chapter 1

Standing Strong and True

COVID-19 has brought a change throughout the entire world as people were forced to adjust to various mandates.

We all have had to adapt to the "new normal" as businesses, government offices, schools, and churches shut their doors, and functioning operations of all kinds shut down everywhere. Hospitals filled, and death tolls increased daily. Health care personnel faced tireless hours along with "essential workers" in every community. Individuals were mandated to isolate themselves in their homes, and relationships with extended family members and friends were restricted. Daily reports, hourly updates, and growing numbers of cases induced fear, rising to the state of near panic.

Fearfulness produced unusual behavior, including the run on toilet tissue, hand sanitizer, paper towels, and all kinds of food products. The shelving in our local stores were bare.

That same fear drove people to cry out to God. Many who had not spoken to him in a while were pleading, "God have mercy." Those living in a relationship with Him recognized that repentance was needed, and many of God's people have committed to do so daily.

In this crisis, we became aware of our spiritual shortcomings. That kind of transparent and honest self-awareness enables us to "Stand firm" during COVID-19 and beyond.

I will confess that in the initial phases of this pandemic, as a believer, my anxieties increased and pushed me deeper into prayer, reading, self-care, and even helped me to maintain my commitment to physical fitness. In addition, it provoked a sense of urgency to constantly examine my relationship with God.

I want to share a couple of the scriptures that have calmed my anxieties and pushed me through it all.

When anxiety was great within me, your consolation brought me joy (Psalms 94:19, NIV).

The Lord has become my fortress, my God the rock in whom I take refuge (Psalm 94:22, NIV).

We can stand strong and true when we are deeply aware of God's mercy and grace, calling us to a transparent self-awareness in which we see both our neediness as well as the awe and wonder of how His heart of grace sees us.

Chapter 2

Where Do You Focus Your Attention?

Scripture: Psalms 37:4 KJV

If you think that is a loaded question, you would be right. One could answer in any of several ways. And the responses from one individual to another could be quite different.

Why is that?

First, everyone responds to such questions from the unique perspectives of their life circumstances. Secondly, some see life and reality only in terms of the natural world. In contrast, others view life through spiritual lenses. And their points of focus will be drastically different. But the differences don't end there. To every man is given the measure of faith (Romans 12:3). For every Christian, the common denominator is Jesus. Yet, some believers have stronger faith and trust than others.

Hebrews 11:6 tells us that "without faith it is impossible to please him; for he that cometh to God must believe that he is, and that he is a rewarder of them that diligently seek him" (KJV).

Faith can and often is impeded by our emotions. Inward emotions such as anger, stress, worry, anxiety, fear, and envy are rooted in our thoughts. Those thoughts drive our emotions, and our emotions will become outwardly evident in our behavior. Where we focus our thoughts and attention reveals our core beliefs.

And left unchecked, those core beliefs with their persistent thoughts and resulting emotions can potentially become destructive to our faith.

But our thoughts and emotions do not need to be left unchecked. God invites us "to cast our cares upon him for he cares for us." He tells us to "Be anxious for nothing" [Ephesians 4:6, KJV] but to make our requests known to him. Anxiety is worry about what is to come that festers in restlessness or fear. God is challenging us to shift our focus from our lack of control to His ultimate control.

Where is your focus?

In Psalm 37, David expresses some concern in the opening verses about how easy it is to be envious of evildoers who seem to live so prosperously. He knows that this is a distraction from where God wants His people to focus. After all, the wicked may put on quite a show, but they're just going to wither and fade, so why be envious of what will not last.

In the greater scheme of things, David declares that we are to focus on the Lord, even take "delight" in Him! To delight yourself in someone means to experience what it is like to know them so deeply that the very thought of spending time with them fills you with pleasure and happiness you can hardly express.

Where do you Focus your attention?

If your attentiveness has been distracted by envy of what others have, then shift your focus. If you are experiencing stress, worry, anxiousness, fear, or any unhelpful thoughts, I challenge you to get into the presence of God. Fix your mind on Jesus. Focus on His goodness, and you will discover what it means to:

1. Fret not (Don't Worry) (v.1).
2. Trust (have confidence) in the Lord and do good, that you may dwell in the land and discover that He is faithful to feed you. (v. 3).

3. Experience God's delight in you as He gives you the very desires (petitions) of your heart in response to your delight in Him (v.4).
4. Fully, unreservedly commit your way to the Lord; trust him to bring those promised requests to pass (v.5).
5. Rest and wait patiently for the Lord, instead of being filled with whining and agonizing (fretting) about the way others, especially the wicked, seemed to have gained so much from their wicked schemes (v. 7).
6. Cease being consumed by anger and wrath or letting those emotions feed your thought of doing something evil for evil doers shall be cut off. Focus and wait on the Lord and the promise that you shall inherit the Earth (v.8-9).

Set your mind on the eternal good things that come from above. Let that be your focus!

> The Lord knows the days of the upright and their inheritance shall be forever. They shall not be ashamed in the evil time: and in the days of famine, they shall be satisfied.
>
> — Psalms 37:19, KJV

Chapter 3

What Will They Say Then?
Scripture: James 4:13-16 KJV

Chadwick Boseman, an American actor, and playwright, especially known for his starring role in Black Panther, left an impressionable mark upon the world locally, nationally, and internationally. In the short span of four years, he rose to the top of his profession before passing with cancer at 43.

The internet and air waves were flooded with the expression of awe and sadness at the news of his passing. Social media was filled with reflections of what was known of his life. Re-runs of the Marvel film Black Panther allowed both the young and seasoned fans to watch their heroic character and, at the same time, realize that their anticipation of Black Panther 2 had come to an unexpected and questionable end.

The sadness felt around the world causes us to remember this:

> Now listen, you who say, "Today or tomorrow we will go to this or that city, spend a year there, carry on business and make money." 14 Why, you do not even know what will happen tomorrow. What is your life? You are a mist that appears for a little while and then vanishes.

—James 4:13-14 NIV

One must be careful about boasting. Be sure that your boasting is in the Lord. Include God in every aspect of your life. The Psalmist declared, "My soul shall make her boast in the LORD: the humble shall hear thereof, and be glad. O magnify the LORD with me, and let us exalt his name together" (Psalms 34:2-3, KJV).

Goals are good, but goals can leave a way for disappointment if we fail to incorporate God in those plans. This is because our future rests in His hands. The Psalmist writes, "So teach us to number our days, that we may apply our hearts to wisdom" (Ps. 90:12, KJV).

Life is short, no matter how long we live. So, do not waste any more time, and please do not be deceived by the thought that you have lots of time remaining to live for God, engage with loved ones, or do what you know you should.

Start today. A choice to begin living wholeheartedly for God points your life in the right direction. It sets your feet on the right path to living out your God-given purpose: that in everything you do, He receives all the glory!

When your journey is over, what will others say then? Chadwick appears to have left a spotless legacy. What about you?

God's desire for your life is the same for all His people: that "He [Christ] might present to himself a glorious church, not having spot, or wrinkle, or any such thing; but that it should be holy and without blemish" (Ephesians 5:27). Let it be said that you did whatever you did, heartily, as to the Lord, and not unto men, knowing that of the Lord you shall receive the reward of the inheritance: for you serve the Lord Christ (Colossians 3:23-24).

Chapter 4

What Will You Do To Know Peace?

Peace is defined (according to the KJV Dictionary/Concordance) as calm repose; eternal rest after death; free of strife or discord; harmony in personal relationships, especially with God.

Peace is a state of mind. The peace we are talking about, like emotions, has a relationship to behavior. Calmness, restfulness, and tranquility impact the way we act.

How many times have you said, "I just want peace and quiet?" By the way, you can't have one without the other. When both peace and quiet exist together, you have emotional balance and a sense of harmony.

Paul writes to the church in Philippians 4:7, "And the peace of God which passeth all understanding, shall keep your hearts and minds through Christ Jesus." The peace to which Paul refers is completely different from peace as the world understands it. This peace surpasses the human idea of a positive attitude or some harmony in a relationship. It reaches well beyond any human relationship. It is far more than a solution to discord.

According to John 14:27, Christ Himself is the source of peace:

"Peace I leave with you, my peace I give unto you: not as the world giveth, give I unto you. Let not your heart be troubled, neither let it be afraid." His peace comes against stress, doubt, fear, and any other forces of this world that rage war within us. God's peace is His antidote for our sin.

Although Christ left the earthly realm, He sent the Holy Ghost, the Comforter that moves into our hearts allowing us to experience peace. This authentic peace comes when we believe, accept, and trust that God is in total control. To maintain His peace, we will not allow our hearts to be troubled and focus instead on the promises of God!

Chapter 5

The Right Heart

Scripture: Psalms 139:19-24 NIV

Life has many cycles.

We all have experienced those events that rotate in and out of our lives, even when they are not always in the same order. Often, we struggle when we are going through one of those cycles because we cannot move forward. We mutter impatiently, "I've been here before," and we begin to feel stagnant.

We may need to be reminded from time to time that the opposite of progression is regression, something we instinctively resist. Some of you may have reached this point in your life after weathering periods of cyclical behavior, perhaps long stagnation. Others may yet be caught in the whirlpool of stagnant living. Some have decided to change and refrain from unhealthy thoughts and behavior that do not produce the growth they now desperately desire.

Have you ever experienced struggling in certain areas of your own life, and you continued to go in circles? Have you faced the frustration of repeated thoughts and behavior that affected you psychologically and spiritually?

A typical example may be how you respond to problems with complaining or anger, perhaps even rage, behaviors that lead to regret. Remember, to grow in God requires an honest and transparent evaluation of yourself.

Looking into a mirror can be uncomfortable, even daunting at times. And what we see in our spiritual mirrors can be even more disturbing. But we must face the truth. Why? You know the answer. "The Lord looks at the heart" (1 Samuel 16:7). And that's not all. The Lord searches the heart in an effort to determine the reward that you shall be given.

In the days of Moses, the men (Israelites) were to be circumcised. Circumcision was a surgery removing the male foreskin. However, God intended for them to go beyond the physical experience and realize a spiritual truth. There needed to be spiritual surgery.

In Deuteronomy 10:16 (AMP), God directed them to "circumcise your heart." His people are to be rid of their sins. And when He adds, "be stiff-necked no longer," He is especially singling out the sins of stubbornness and obstinance. In other words, God desires total submission both inwardly and outwardly.

Let your self-awareness be genuinely transparent. Do not close your eyes to your stiff-necked stubbornness, your obstinate refusal to submit to His spiritual surgery in your life. When your heart is right with God, it changes how you interact with people and how you choose to act in the relationships with those you encounter. Those choices will reflect the message that God is Love! How you treat yourself as well as others will change when your heart is right!

David knew that God searched the heart, and his love for God changed how he saw others. His attitude even toward his enemies changed as he realized that his enemies were also God's enemies.

But we must beware of our natural feelings. The actions we may want to take may feel justified. Vengeance and mercy belong to God. Christ articulates that God "rains on the just as well as the unjust" (Matthew 5:45). That truth helps us understand why we are not to hate people but the sin only. We are to love everyone!

In David's initial and natural perspective, he spoke words of hatred toward those he felt spoke wickedly about God and used His name in vain. "For they speak against thee wickedly, and thine enemies take thy name in vain (misuse). Do not I hate them, O Lord, that hate thee? and am not I grieved with those that rise up against thee? I hate them with perfect hatred: I count them mine enemies" (Psalm 139:21-22, KJV). Our natural responses do not reflect God's point of view.

Have you noticed those Facebook posts that start with "Blessed and Highly Favored," "God is Good," and by the end, there is BLUURRP? It blows my mind that someone can associate God with such language so foreign to His heart of love in the same breath!

Just as hate is taught, a heart that is set right with the love of God teaches us to pray for others, including praying sincerely for God's enemies as well as our own, instead of judging them.

And if that were not enough, Jesus told us, "Love your enemies, bless them that curse you, do good to them that hate you, and pray for them which despitefully use you, and persecute you" (Matthew 5:44, NIV).

The right heart will stop you from falling out with people. The heart that is right with God and filled with His love is totally submitted to the work of the Spirit of God within You. He will cause you to sense the conviction that He brings to you, and He will enable you to navigate through that conviction to experience His loving hand of correction. The heart set right breathes deeply of His correction and chooses to refrain from the old, stiff-necked stubborn and obstinate behavior and like David ask God, "Search me, O God, and know my heart: try me, and know my thoughts: And see if there be any wicked way in me, and lead me in the way everlasting" (Psalm 139:23,24).

The right heart is willing to let the Spirit remove the foreskin of sin from your heart and submit to the change He wants to bring to your life.

Chapter 6

In Reflection, There Are Great Gains

Scripture: Psalm 103:1-5

This has been a wild year!

Many have had so many emotions, thoughts, blessings, tests, and trials and tribulations. For our church's bishops and pastors, it has been a year that caused us to constantly pivot and shift our attention from one time to another. Most of all, this has been a journey of faith as never before.

We could call this the year of "reflective perspective."

I can remember celebrating my birthday in our worship service on January 26, 2020, surrounded by those I love and who love me back. Then there was the short journey after the service to have a peaceful, even blissful dinner.

We learned that what was peace-filled for us turned out to be sudden destruction for others during the year. There was the day that my friends and I heard the daunting news of Kobe Bryant's death along with his children. We all stood around chattering numbly. We were texting, searching the internet, and scanning news feeds informing us of a helicopter crash. Kobe, his daughter Gigi and seven others, including the pilot, were gone. The breathtaking tragedy was felt around the world.

While we were processing this news, we began hearing the yet sketchy news of the coronavirus (COVID-19). Then came the months filled with the elections, reports of hate crimes, images of riots, inequities, injustices, hospitalizations, and death tolls worldwide.

In the face of all that, we hear the words of James telling us that we should "count it all joy when you fall into divers [old English for diverse] temptations knowing that the testing of your faith worketh patience. But let patience have its perfect work, that you may be perfect and entire wanting nothing" (James 1:2-4).

Psychologists and counselors tell us that reflection means to examine our state of mind, our thoughts, and our feelings in light of our circumstances. Paul writes to Corinth that in Christ, we are reminded to reflect or examine our souls: "Examine yourselves, whether ye be in the faith; prove your own selves. Know ye not your own selves, how that Jesus Christ is in you, except ye be reprobates" – [i.e., fail to meet the test] (2nd Corinthians 13:5, KJV).

I believe it is high time to be about our Father's business. As we reflect on the past year, we are aware that we must still wear our outward masks, but it is time that we remove our inner emotional and spiritual masks! We need to enter a new season in which the spirit-man is subject to the Spirit of God's maintenance work to better enable us to do our work of faith.

In Psalms 90:12, we find a poetic prayer by Moses seeking God to "teach us to number our days, that we apply our hearts unto wisdom" (KJV). His words paint a prodding picture that life is indeed short! Perhaps we should follow Moses' prayer with one of our own, asking God to help us not waste the precious time we have. Life is as brief as a vapor!"

Taking time to reflect on our lives should cause us to use our time more wisely, particularly with a renewed awareness of eternity and God's Kingdom.

There are truly great gains in the reflections of a heart fixed on God and His Kingdom!

I believe that many of us can attest that in this year of 2020, learning to be flexible and change direction in moments has allowed us to stand steady and strong. But, if you have not known how to shift and change at the promptings of the Spirit, you have indeed been given that chance in these past 16 months!

We can stand strong because God Himself is our Sure Foundation. We have only made it through this past year because He is our very present help in times of trouble. By His invitation, we have dined with Him at the table of His grace and mercy.

We can face life's struggles because God's word can be trusted. David wrote, "My voice shalt thou hear in the morning, O LORD; in the morning will I direct my prayer unto thee, and will look up (Psalm 5:3).

Throughout David's psalms, we discover the value of gaining knowledge and understanding. In 2 Timothy 3:16, we are reminded that "all scripture is given by inspiration of God, and is profitable for doctrine, for reproof, for correction, for instruction in righteousness" (NIV). But there is more. Proverbs reveals that Wisdom is the voice of God, the Rhema, that brings personal clarity to the knowledge and understanding we gain from the scriptures.

I've seen some who have matured and some who have remained stagnant. I have watched some fall away and others who have returned home to their faith. Yet, I have remained optimistic! My physical sight may have begun to blur. Still, I am thankful God has allowed me to see with a Rhema clarity vicariously through His eyes.

After all, "faith is the substance of things hoped for and the evidence of things not seen" (Hebrew 11:1, KJV). To see what is not presently visible is to see as God sees. Eyes of faith are centered on the Goodness of God, allowing us to truly delight in Him. As we meditate on His word day and night, His Rhema fills us with courage, inviting us to cast all our cares on Him.

God is our rock, our fortress, our high tower, and our strength.

He is more than ABLE to do exceedingly above what you can ask or think!

A special note from the author:

As this chapter was being written, 2020 was ending. We are preparing to step into the unknown of 2021. My prayer is that as each reader faces the transitions of life, you will "keep the faith!"

Stand strong in the name of Jesus. Let the banner over your life declare that God is good!

In these past months, I have adopted Psalm 103:2-5 for the year to come. I have chosen and continue to choose to bless His holy name with all that is within me! I choose to take care and not forget all His benefits. I choose to be filled with thankfulness that our God of love forgives all my iniquities and heals all my diseases. He redeems my life from destruction and crowns me with lovingkindness and tender mercies. He alone satisfies my mouth with good things; so that my youth is renewed like the eagle.

Stop and reflect. Ask yourself, "What have I gained through the hard times?"

Chapter 7

The Mind Is A Terrible Thing To Waste

Scripture: Psalms 143:4-10

While no one knows where the mind is located, we understand that it has three distinct functions: 1) Intellect: the ability to think and reason; 2) Sensibility: the capacity to feel and be aware; and 3) Will: the power to choose.

Nehemiah leads us to understand that it takes a firm mindset to accomplish goals, especially when the task is more complicated. Nehemiah determined that the wall around Jerusalem could be built because the people had a mind to work. "So, built we the wall; and all the wall was joined together unto the half thereof: for the people had a mind to work" (Nehemiah 4:6, KJV). The word "so" is a conjunction that bridges clauses in the same sentence together. It means "as a result," and in this case, due to the peoples' commitment, the work of building the wall was accomplished. Not only did the people have a mind to work, but they had a mindset of resilience, even when facing opposition. Once they were guided through the process to change their outlook from having no hope to one of optimism, they could show resolve. Someone said, "You can achieve what your mindset perceives." Have you ever been in a situation that seemed bleak and grim, so grim you struggled to have hope?

Yet God always has a way of bringing us out of the fog of hopelessness, and not only does he bring us out, but He renews our minds, establishes our steps, and directs our paths. In his song of faith, David testifies of God's power and protection: "Blessed is the Lord, who daily loadeth us with benefits, even the God of our salvation" (Psalm 68:19, KJV). And one of those benefits is that He is with us, bearing our burdens.

When God knows that we trust Him enough to truly guard our hearts and minds, to fix our minds on Him completely, He chooses to pour His benefits into our lives. The prophet Isaiah wrote, "You will keep in perfect peace those whose minds are steadfast, because they trust in you." (Is 26:3, NIV). Perfect peace may be the greatest benefit of all as we live in right relationship with Him.

Life is a spiritual battle that many seem to be losing, yet the victory has already been won. When His perfect peace is missing, our minds become damaged. Our ability to think and reason (our intellect), our capacity to feel and be aware (our sensibility), and our power to choose (our will) all become distorted. The mind that does not have perfect peace produces behavior that does not reflect God's authority and nature. And to be sure, this is true even among those in Christian communities.

We must maintain our focus on God. We must trust Him rather than lean on our own understanding. In other words, we must acknowledge Him in all our ways. The heart and mind that is centered on Him will experience His benefits.

Once again, we turn to the words of the psalmist:

> Therefore, is my spirit overwhelmed within me; my heart within me is desolate. I remember the days of old; I meditate on all thy works; I muse on the work of thy hands. I stretch forth my hands unto thee: my soul thirsteth after thee, as a thirsty land. Selah.
>
> Hear me speedily, O Lord: my spirit faileth: hide not thy face

from me, lest I be like unto them that go down into the pit. Cause me to hear thy lovingkindness in the morning; for in thee do I trust: cause me to know the way wherein I should walk; for I lift up my soul unto thee.

Deliver me, O Lord, from mine enemies: I flee unto thee to hide me. Teach me to do thy will; for thou art my God: thy spirit is good; lead me into the land of uprightness.

— Psalm 143:4-10, KJV

As David is on the run from his enemies, he cries out to God. Feeling as if his spirit was failing, David longs to hear God "speedily." He earnestly petitions God for deliverance from his enemies. He seeks to hide himself in God.

In this crisis, David realizes that he could not get himself out of this pit. He needs God to spare him physically and restore him emotionally. In times of fear, stress, worry, hopelessness, anxiety, and depression, we need to choose to be transparent with God. Even though David remembered the days of old, meditated on the works of God's hand, he knew that he was losing control as if he were wrapped in darkness.

David's example should cause us to be cautious. Those with hearts in the right relationship with God must indeed be in tune with their inner self. Saints are falling away from God and failing to be transparent before Him. Be aware, and alert others that the masking season is over! God sees through the masks anyway.

Keep your mind fixed on what is eternal and righteous. When you need help to stay focused, simply ask. Please, do not suffer in silence while support is in plain sight.

A mind is a terrible thing to waste!

Chapter 8

Run and Tell

Scripture: Isaiah 41:10 KJV

Sometimes, even when our intentions are good, the things we tell others may not be correct. We give wrong directions, get times mixed up, and share information to discover later that the facts were all screwed up.

That can be a serious problem when we want to help someone. We can fail to be discerning about the situation and the timing and do more harm than good. We are told to seize the moment, but it must be the right moment.

An old quote is attributed to Oscar Wilde and Will Rogers: "You never get a second chance to make a first impression." There are no do-overs. The things we say or do can leave a bad impression of ourselves or someone we represent, and worse, we may damage others.

But with God and His grace, we are allowed to change. The impression that others may have of us does not have to be the lasting one. What do I mean? When your behavior proceeds you, you often end up with a less than desirable reputation. Soon people can be heard saying things like, "he ain't never gonna change."

And of course, people can spend months and even years trying to convince themselves and others that they have, in fact, really changed. People can even add that they have changed since God has come into their lives. But others need to be able to see the change for themselves. If they are to know that your claims are valid, they will need to see new behavior and hear the difference for themselves.

Since the beginning, God has identified His people as a "chosen generation." "Who has done this and carried it through, calling forth the generations from the beginning? I, the LORD—with the first of them and with the last—I am he" (Isaiah 41:4, NIV). He has known us from the beginning of the foundation of the world.

Look at Abraham. He found favor with God, and God chose Abraham as a friend. But let us also remember that Abraham proved himself to be a friend of God. "But thou Israel are my servant, Jacob whom I have chosen, the seed of Abraham my friend" (Isaiah 41:8), KJV).

What about your friendship with God today?

We must take note that God chose His people not because they deserved it but simply because He desired to do so.

For you are a people, holy to the Lord your God. The Lord, your God, has chosen you out of all the peoples on the face of the earth to be his people, his treasured possession.

The Lord did not set his affection on you and chose you because you were more numerous than other peoples, for you were the fewest of all peoples. But it was because the Lord loved you and kept the oath. He swore to your ancestors that he brought you out with a mighty hand and redeemed you from the land of slavery, from the power of Pharaoh, king of Egypt.

After the Lord your God has driven them out before you, do not say to yourself, "The Lord has brought me here to take possession of this land because of my righteousness." No, it is on account of the wickedness of these nations that the Lord is going to drive them out before you. It is not because of your righteousness or your integrity that you are going in to take possession of their land. But on account of the wickedness of these nations, the Lord your God will drive them out before you to accomplish what he swore to your fathers, to Abraham, Isaac, and Jacob.

Understand, then, that it is not because of your righteousness that the Lord your God is giving you this good land to possess, for you are a stiff-necked people.

(Deuteronomy 7:7-8; 9:4-6, NIV).

Israel's reputation as a stiff-necked people is easy for us to grasp in light of their behavior. Thankfully, what God has spoken about the "former generation" applies to us as well. God will be with us, and because He is faithful to his word, we have the opportunity to represent him well as His chosen people in this present age. He has not cast us away, but instead, he has chosen us to be His servants. So, we must go and faithfully tell the world of the goodness of the Lord.

The next time you are given an opportunity to pour into someone, take care and refrain from talking about yourself and your problems. Instead, encourage the lost to choose a life sheltered in the safety of the Lord. Never forget your friendship with Him and what He wants you to do:

1. Fear Not. He is With You.
2. Run and tell someone. Do not be dismayed because God is my God.
3. Tell them God will strengthen them, for the joy of the Lord Is their strength
4. God will Help You. He is a present help in the time of trouble.
5. God will uphold you with the right hand of His righteousness, not your righteousness but His.

Do not miss the opportunities God gives us to be witnesses for Him! Be a stable, unwavering, predictable, and thoroughly trustworthy friend living and speaking the truth in love! Run and tell.

Chapter 9

Thank You, God, For The Invitation

Scripture: John 4:21-26

This past Sunday, I was reminded of the story about the Samaritan woman who came to draw water at Jacob's well.

Although Jewish in ancestry, Samaritans had married non-Jews and were considered inferior and generally despised by "pure Jews." Jews were known to travel miles out of their way to avoid Samaria because Samaritans were a mixed race. As it has been for ages, prejudice and bigotry are not new.

This Samaritan woman was also experiencing prejudice of another kind. She had gone to the well later than the others in the town because she was a woman living in sin and the other women wanted nothing to do with her.

To make this moment even more stressful, a Jew spoke to her at the well. Jews found Samaritans so distasteful that they would not even talk to them. And Jewish men would have nothing at all to do with Samaritan women.

But this was Jesus! And He sees the world from a different perspective. He is God manifested in the flesh, and the gospel He came to proclaim is for everyone!

Just think where you were when you first encountered God, or more correctly, when God encountered you! This woman was at Jacob's well at about "the sixth hour" or noon, but the real issue is where she was spiritually at that exact moment. She knew she was morally loose, so she avoided the other women. And that is the same issue for each of us.

And what barriers does God break to get to us?

Christ, of course, came from heaven to earth, but notice that Jesus is not put off by social or racial, or class barriers. And most of all, He is not put off by the barrier of our sinfulness. He ate with Publicans and spent time with tax collectors; both were hated people of His day. Jesus already knew of this woman's repeated adultery and the Jews and Samaritans' prejudice toward each other but still interacted with her.

When the woman of Samaria met Jesus, He was resting at the well after a long journey, just waiting patiently for her. I believe that your blessing of hope and forgiveness is waiting for you to come by as well. Perhaps you need a change in your circumstances. But remember, you need God to change you first, then your situation!

For this Samaritan woman, this particular encounter was both an introduction and an invitation. She was introduced to Him, not because she was looking for Him, but because He sought her out just as He does with all of us.

That encounter then led to an invitation. In this familiar setting, Jesus guides the conversation and eventually invites her to drink not from the physical well but from a spiritual well that would never run dry.

While this well of life was a gift from God, she had to first become aware of the One who was offering it to her. Like her, we cannot experience this gift of God without first discovering the Giver Himself. We must have a divine encounter with Jesus.

When Jesus reaches out to us, and we stop for a moment to listen, our interest is piqued, giving us the chance to gain insight. Our fresh understanding allows us to make the right decision.

Thank God for my invitation to salvation through Christ!

Regardless of my ethnicity, where I live, my social/financial status, my education, my sins, and flaws, plus all my hang-ups, hookups, or mix-ups, He chose to invite me to drink freely of the water from His well of life, to experience what it means never to thirst again wanting for nothing! And this well has become a spring of everlasting life.

God knows us and looks on the inward part, so we cannot hide who we are from Him. This woman could not hide who she was. Jesus knew about her sins, her five husbands, and the one she was living with at that time. But notice that Jesus did not ask her to move out or change her address. He did not mention how she had avoided others and told her to get her image in the community set straight. His discussion with her was not some refined interaction admonishing her to reform. Still, it was a raw invitation to experience the touch of God. He offered her a drink from His well of life and grace and invited her to discover what it means to enter into true worship.

We can see from this story that when God seeks to encounter us, it does not matter where we are, who we are, or when it happens. Unfortunately, too many assume that we will experience our encounter with God in church on Sunday morning. But the place we worship is not as significant as the attitude in which we worship!

Is your worship genuine and real?

But the hour cometh, and now is, when the true worshippers shall worship the Father in spirit and in truth: for the Father seeketh such to worship him. God is a Spirit: and they that worship him must worship him in spirit and in truth (John 4:23-24, KJV).

Chapter 10

Look Who Is At The Table

Scripture: Psalms 23:5

Discovering the practice of self-control

The bible refers to the day in which we live as perilous times. These are truly evil days, undeniably the end times.

And how quickly the time seems to fly. The pace of life has brought us flared tempers. We have seen a noticeable spike in mental health diagnoses, climbing divorce rates, and people who seem unable to get along.

Murders are becoming more and more common. Wrong is being defined as right and right as wrong. Mankind has become lovers of themselves as well as carried away by their own lust and deceit. Mothers and daughters are envious of one another, and fathers are hated by their sons.

Yet, in such terrible times, we as the people of God are to possess His love and be possessed by His love. God is Love. Love is His name! And those around us need to see His love in us so that they can see more of God and less of us.

Paul warns Timothy that these times will come and will continue until the second coming of Christ.

"But mark this: There will be terrible times in the last days. People will be lovers of themselves, lovers of money, boastful, proud, abusive, disobedient to their parents, ungrateful, unholy, without love, unforgiving, slanderous, without self-control, brutal, not lovers of the good, treacherous, rash, conceited, lovers of pleasure rather than lovers of God having a form of godliness but denying its power.

Have nothing to do with such people [KJV says "from such turn away"]. They are the kind who worm their way into homes and gain control over gullible women, who are loaded down with sins and are swayed by all kinds of evil desires, always learning but never able to come to a knowledge of the truth." (2 Timothy 3:1-7. NIV).

Paul speaks with a passionate sense of urgency in these verses when he warns against superficial Christianity.

Remember, we read the word of God to gain:

1. Godly principles
2. Truth and understanding
3. Direction and correction
4. His will for our lives

In times like these, each of us needs an ever-increasing urgency to experience life "in Christ," through which we exercise self-control through prayer and supplication.

Self-control is one of the nine fruits of the Spirit recorded in Galatians 5:23. Self-control is the ability to control oneself emotionally and behaviorally. For Christians, we do not learn to live that way by our willpower but by the ministry of God's Spirit.

One that proclaims the indwelling Spirit of God must be a willing vessel that allows the Spirit to evidence His fruit, especially in difficult times.

You can certainly tell a tree by the fruit it bears! Someone has said, "Having this good defense mechanism is profitable for your positive, spiritual, and natural development and growth!"

David learned to practice self-control with the Lord as his

shepherd. He was able to write his psalms from his experience as a shepherd. As sheep follow the shepherd, he depicts us as willingly following our Great Shepherd and experiencing the spiritual rest as "he lies me down in green pastures" (Psalm 23:2, KJV). The Lord will lead and guide the sheep that desire to follow Him and be led into a life of righteousness.

This is the way of discipleship. As He leads us, He longs to equip us with the necessary tools of discipleship. As His disciples, we submit, commit, comply, obey, and follow the Shepherd. In one sense, this is a life of self-control in which we choose to do as He wants. And on the other hand, this is a life defined by His control to which we submit.

God did not promise that all our paths would be easy, but He promised to take the lead and to "lead us in the paths of righteousness for his name's sake" (v.3). Because He leads me, by faith, I can understand that the Lord as my Shepherd lovingly "prepares the table before me in the presence of my enemies." As He "anoints my head with oil and my cup runneth over" (v. 5), I exercise self-control and submit to His blessing. And if that were not enough, the Good Shepherd will protect me: "Surely goodness and mercy shall follow me all the days of my life and I will dwell in the house of the Lord forever" (v. 6).

Stop making excuses for poor behavior and misconduct!

You already know that your adversary is on the prowl. Yet, look who is at the table with you. Get ahead of the curve and practice self-control in every area of your life. We must all have a level of Godly and Christlike maturity when it's time to face our enemies.

In Him, we can be at peace. At the table of God's grace and peace, there is rest.

Chapter 11

Poor and Ineffective Communication Destroys Relationships

Scripture: Ephesians 4:29-32 (KJV)

Let no corrupting talk come out of your mouths, but only such as is good for building up, as fits the occasion, that it may give grace to those who hear.

How many times have you experienced a thriving relationship that comes to a sour end? It may have been a long-term relationship or a short-term one, but you know in your heart of hearts that the relationship did not have to end on the sour note that it did.

You may have had a longtime friend, a colleague, or business partner; a sister, a cousin, an aunt, or uncle; it could have been a church friend, a best friend, a boyfriend, or a husband. But, despite your best efforts, you reached a point of being muted strangers. The unreconcilable differences are undeniable, and the struggle to regain that interpersonal relationship you once enjoyed has been choked out by the inability to communicate effectively.

Effective communication is a must in any relationship. You must be purposefully present both cognitively and emotionally to listen, understand and interact meaningfully. "Let your speech be always with grace, seasoned with salt, that ye may know how ye ought to answer every man" (Colossians 4:6, KJV). Paul's words help us understand that in spreading the message of Jesus Christ, we must be gracious in all our relationships. We need to recognize that we are effective as we speak the truth with courtesy and respect. Someone has said, "Say what it is your saying nicely!"

The word of God teaches us not to be deceived: evil communications corrupt good manners (1st Corinthians 15:33, KJV). Paul is educating the church of Corinth and other Christians abroad to be careful about how we relate to others, in particular unbelievers. We must ensure that what we say does not result in or is misunderstood, causing some to waver from their faith. Remember that the devil is always there to steal and to kill and to destroy (John 10:10, KJV).

For several generations, the children of Israel did not hear from God. They had turned away from Him, and He chose not to communicate with them. We all know how it feels when we can't hear from our Creator and Father.

Just as we speak about the eyes being the windows to the soul, our ears are the gateways through which we hear the truth. And just as we are to guard what we hear and avoid being deceived, distracted, or discouraged, so it is with our mouths whereby we declare with the power of death and life as we speak.

Paul warns us not to give into bad language or express inappropriate attitudes or meanness. We must not exhibit anger or express desires that are not of God. By such attitudes, we grieve the Holy Spirit. Instead, we are to be kind one to another, tenderhearted, forgiving one another as Christ forgave us.

Here are some things to ponder! Relationships do not have to end on sour notes if we learn to...

1. ...be aware of our insecurities, address them, and check our own biases.
2. ...gain the necessary confidence to have "hard conversations" yet in love.

3. ...recognize that in these "hard conversations," emotions must not drive what we say. Instead, you should deal with your emotions before speaking with others.
4. ...be of good courage. Do not allow situations to fester. Deal with them and beware of avoidance.
5. ...avoid giving in to fight or flight. Learn to Reason. You cannot allow your feelings to drive or override your reason. Practice self-control and be patient.
6. ...not allow everything you hear to perplex you. Everyone has their perception of truth. As a believer, the One who is Truth is your Shepherd. Follow Him.
7. ...be willing to be wrong sometimes. Yes! Because, as surprising as it may seem, you are not always right.
8. ...be honest and kind, even supportive whenever you can.
9. ...be willing to forgive and to ask for forgiveness.
10. ...be open-minded and willing to listen. If you are talking, you cannot listen.
11. ...do not be easily OFFENDED or jump over into defense. Get control of your emotions. Have a clear train of thought and forgo the tendency to respond with "I feel ."
12. ...consider your sources and remind yourself that the information you have may not be complete. Don't elevate the tone of your interactions. Everything is not a war.
13. ...be willing to engage responsively. Abhor the "shutdowns" (i.e., accusations, awkward communication, and the loose-lipped expression "Well I heard. "
14. ...clarify someone's choice of words or expressions. When in doubt, ask questions with respect and an honest attempt to understand and respond effectively. Never appear or sound sarcastic.

Grow from the past. Failed relationships can reveal the need to effectively communicate your needs, wants, and desires and enable you to respond to others harmoniously.

Seek to resolve matters with the love and the mind of Christ.

Chapter 12

Lord, Keep On Keeping Me

Scripture: 2nd Corinthians 12:7-9

By His grace, we are saved by faith. It is not of our own. But it is a gift from God. A gift that keeps on giving.

In our need, God chose to bail us out. That act of love is a debt we all owe but can never repay. Yes! We can choose to do our reasonable service, but it will never measure up to the sacrifice of the Lamb slain before the foundation of the world. Furthermore, God keeps on giving, so how will we truly ever repay Him?

The grace extended to us saved us from sin. For those who have come to Christ, the washing away of sins means that we have been reconciled to Him.

But His grace is not for just a moment. It is a continuation, and that truth shifts the focus from Savior to Sustainer. God's grace gave us life but also continues to sustain us.

Lord, keep on keeping me.

David says to "Cast thy burden upon the Lord, and he will sustain thee: he shall never suffer the righteous to be moved" (Psalms 55:22, KJV). God will sustain you, keep, comfort, encourage, strengthen, support, and assist you; what joy to know that He will be there to help you.

God allows us to delight ourselves in the Lord. The word reminds us that "God is our refuge and a very present help in the time of trouble" (Psalms 46:1).

We all will see trouble around us, but God is our Sustainer, and He is right here with us in the midst of it all.

In light of all the destruction, isolation, sickness, disease, and plague around me, it is a true blessing to be able to rely on the One I know and is in me. When you can reflect on the miracles, signs, and wonders of God, you can realize anew that He is indeed God Everlasting.

I like to say that God is the only constant in my life, for He never changes, and He is always present. He is attentive to my heart, cry, spirit, mind, soul, and being. As the song says, "searched all over, couldn't find nobody, nobody is Greater nor like our God." So, because He is the God whose deeds and continued grace have proven His faithfulness, I say, "Lord, keep on keeping me."

I have had several calls this week about the outbreak of COVID affecting various family members, including my son's team member at his university. The week has been filled with making phone calls to check in on loved ones' progress, praying with them, offering words of encouragement and services to be rendered. I have listened to their various experiences from one extreme to the other. Some symptoms range from mild to nearly nothing, but others experienced extreme incapacitation and even struggled with their mental state. Some even uttered, "I felt like giving up."

The scripture tells us that the enemy desires to have you and sift you as wheat until nothing is left and blow you away. "O, what a blessed assurance" it is when you truly have your relationship with God. You may recognize Him for who He is by the power of His might, but in your weakness, you struggle to pray for yourself. But the Lord God Himself can pray for you as he prayed for Peter "that thy faith fail not" (Luke 22:31).

I was recently reminded of Paul. I thought of how he prayed and asked God to remove his "thorn in the flesh." Three times he asked. I was reminded of Jesus' petitions in the Garden of Gethsemane. Three times and three different ways, He asked God, if it is the will of God, to allow this cup to pass from him.

In both situations – Paul's request and Jesus' petition – God does not grant their requests. For Jesus, the Father does not remove the cup; and for Paul, God does not take the thorn from his "flesh." Yet, they both remained faithful in their afflictions and carried out their missions designed by God. Because of their examples, this one thing I know and will hold on to, that His grace is sufficient for me "for His strength is made perfect in weakness" (v.9).

For us, He has not taken COVID-19 away. Yet, I will hold on to the sustaining power and the grace of God, thanking him and declaring:

"Lord, keep on keeping me."

What about You?

Chapter 13

Protective Custody

Scripture: Psalms 18:2-3

Everybody is familiar with the words "protective custody." Hopefully, they have heard them in the movies or a news report. But some have faced them in their lives or the lives of their family or friends.

The custody, of course, is in the hands of law enforcement. And as necessary as it is supposed to be, many individuals do not want to be in protective custody. They find the restrictions to be a hassle and feel distressed at how it disrupts their lives, even though the idea is to keep them from being hurt or worse.

Spiritually, God offers us His protection. All we have to do is submit to His custody. His purpose is to protect us from the harmful actions of others and our own harmful choices.

God's protective custody is always at work for our own good. I'm reminded of the song "I'm Safe in His Arms."

> When the storms, when the storms of life
>   Are raging and the billows roll
>   I'm glad He shall hide me safe in His arms

— Rev. Milton Brunson

Moses, when he found himself starring at the burning bush that was not being turned to ashes, God spoke to him and revealed to Moses that He was the great "I AM." The One who would protect him as he returned to Egypt to set His people free. After the exodus, the great "Coming Out" from the years of slavery, Moses still depended on God's protective hand.

The journey of obedience allowed Moses to discover more about his Protector. In Exodus 17, the army of Israel faced a battle against an enemy king named Amalek. In preparation for the battle, Moses sends Joshua to the men who would battle him. While the army of Israel was engaged in combat, Moses, Aaron, and Hur were at the top of a mountain overlooking the battlefield.

At God's direction, Moses was to take the shepherd's staff that God has turned into a snake back at the burning bush and hold it up during the battle. This staff has special importance because on this occasion and ever after, what had been the staff of Moses was called the rod of God!

And it came to pass when Moses held high the rod of God in his hand, Israel prevailed: and when he let down his hand, Amalek prevailed. In the end, the army of Israel prevailed by the power and protection of God. Although Moses had times of weakness and his arms grew weary, Aaron and Hur, who were with him, got a large stone for Moses to sit on, and they stood at his side and lifted his hands with the rod of God raised high. And the scripture says that "his hands were steady until the going down of the sun (v.13). And the victory belonged to God's people. When the battle was over, Moses built an altar to God, who has revealed to him that one of His names is Jehovah Nissi, which is interpreted as "The LORD-Is-My-Banner." You see, when an army or a group of people wanted others to know who they were, they traveled under a banner or flag, sometimes called a standard, that identified the king under whom they lived and served and enjoyed protection.

When we face battles in the journey of our lives, God Himself is our Jehovah Nisei, the banner of His authority and our protector. Therefore, we look to Him to give us spiritual victories. No wonder the Apostle Paul wrote, "Thanks be to God! He gives us the victory through the Lord Jesus Christ" (1 Corinthians 15:57 NIV).

Who wouldn't want to live under the banner of God's authority? He is the One who not only protects us but fights for us as well. He even promised Israel to war against Amalek from generation to generation (v.16). This means that the Amalekites in our lives will never have victory over us because I AM protects us indefinitely.

I think I'll stay in His protective custody, where I have the privilege of living under the Banner through Christ Jesus. Under His protection, I am "in the hand of God, never to perish, neither shall any man pluck me out of his hand" (John 10:28). And not only do I enjoy His protection in this life, but under His authority, He grants me eternal life. "For to be absent from the body is to be present with the Lord." (2 Corinthians 5:8). God's protection for His people has no limits and no boundaries. It's reckless. We can't: lose. He is always fighting for us, and we stay in His protection. Psalm 18:2-3 records for us the ways that God protected David:

1. He is my rock that cannot be penetrated.
2. My fortress, place of safety
3. My buckler, my shield that mediates between me and harm.
4. The horn of my salvation, representing God's might and power.
5. My high tower, a tower that is high above my enemies.

David was filled with gratitude for the deliverance and victory he experienced through God's banner of protection. He praised God and called on Him for his continued protection!

How many of us will choose to remain in the protective custody of God our Banner? How many will like David in (v. 5) will "call upon the Lord, for he is worthy to be praised: so shall I be saved from my enemies."

My choice: God is over my life!

Chapter 14

Reset, Impact, Team Selection
Scripture: Ruth 1:16-18, ESV

In December 2019, God gave me a message that I preached entitled "Reset to Restart." We know that, in reality, we cannot go back and change what has already happened. But God has the ability to make our crooked paths straight. He is the Alpha and Omega. The I AM is always present. He is there at the beginning, and He will be there at the end.

It is a great consolation to know that "Jesus Christ[is] the same yesterday, and today, and forever" (Hebrews 13:8). In Him, I can reset to restart.

This past year has been a time in which we have had to reset. These months have allowed many to sleep in a bit later, work from home, go to school from home, church hop from home, shop from home, even have medical appointments from home. This reset time has afforded some of us a measure of financial gain, perhaps a chance to launch a new business or even see our families restored. And the list can go on and on.

When you stop to think of the goodness of Jesus, we realize that the reset has allowed us to choose to draw near unto God that He, in turn, will draw near unto us. During this reset, each of us has had a personal time for self-examination, repentance, correction, spiritual enlightenment as well as spiritual growth. To those who have chosen to be part of the shift, we have been invited to embrace a new sensitivity to the Spirit of God. The reset has opened ways to disseminate the Gospel of Jesus Christ to the masses through the airways, new use of technology, and social networking. The ministry has been taken outside of the church walls.

Our first reaction to all this change may have troubled us. But after we have had time to recast these months' events, we have seen the challenges of the reset as real advantages and opportunities for impact. There is an impact on each of our lives as we have rediscovered how we can impact others and be a light to them. We have a new awareness that others are watching us. We must ask ourselves honestly, "Have we drawn people to the Light of the World," or have we driven them away from ourselves and the Light they should have seen in us.

The Old Testament characters Ruth and Naomi come to mind. Their lives impacted Boaz, and the result was a blessing to all three of them. Likewise, our lives' impact starts with the bond we form with others who see our relationship with God. Then, at some point, they are drawn to commit themselves to their relationship with God.

This opportunity to impact others in this time of reset is much more effective when we are bonded with others who share this same desire. This time of reset and impact calls for a time of "team selecting." As the Bishop under whom my ministry is blessed recently preached, we should pick our "team" wisely.

This should not be based on our feelings, not based on years of relationships or blood relationships. These choices must be made prayerfully and skillfully. These kinds of bonds must be with individuals who choose and are committed to loyalty in this relationship.

For example, in my leadership role of ministry, I must be "instant in season and out of season," always equipped to deliver the Word of God. That includes times when individuals want to hear and when they do not. This also includes times of rebuke, always speaking the truth in love. One's feelings cannot influence such times. Since we are all called to give direction and prayerfully confront someone lovingly, we must have those with us in this team ministry who can receive direction and correction.

And it is undoubtedly wise to select teammates that have firm faith and a holy ambition. They need to have the drive, zeal, motivation, ability to handle the truth, be dependable, secure, confident, serious, ability to think critically, and be the kind of person who does not drain everything from you but can deposit in you additional strength and faith.

In the earlier example of Naomi and Ruth, Naomi suffered a significant loss with the death of her husband and both of her sons and then faced the responsibility of caring for her daughter-in-law Ruth. Feeling that God was dealing bitterly with her, Naomi returned home to Bethlehem with Ruth, a Moabite, and a foreigner to Bethlehem. Note that in verse 21, Naomi speaks that when she left Bethlehem those many years before, she was "full." Still, when the Lord led her home again, she came "empty," alone with no family other than a Moabitess daughter-in-law.

And when we look at the rest of this story, we can have hope during our times of reset. In this time of transition, we read that Naomi's life had a real impact on Ruth. When they had been left alone in Moab, Ruth had bonded so intensely with Naomi that she chose to go to a foreign land with her mother-in-law rather than stay in her own home area.

Listen to Ruth's own words to Naomi: (v.16) "Do not urge me to leave you or to return from following you. For where you go I will go, and where you lodge I will lodge. Your people shall be my people, and you're God my God. (v.17) Where you die I will die, and there will I be buried. May the Lord do so to me and more also if anything but death parts me from you" (v.18). When Naomi saw that Ruth was determined to go with her, she said nothing more.

Ruth's choice to stay with Naomi and Naomi's choice to keep

Ruth with her had an eternal impact because Ruth became the great-grandmother of King David through whose lineage Jesus was born into the world as Savior and King of all Kings.

As we search for those who will serve with us, may we have the sensitivity of Naomi to recognize the Ruths in our paths which God has placed before us as "keepers." Our lives will be stronger with them, and our ministry will be fruitful.

And we should ask ourselves, "Can others authentically say the same about us?"

In this period of reset, let's trust God to perfect the steps and plans of our lives and let us have an impact for His glory (see Psalm 138:8).

Chapter 15

Negativity Is Contagious

Scripture: Psalms 118:5, 24 KJV

Negativity is like a nasty germ.

Think about that scratchy throat, the sneezing, or even that discreet cough. If there is one cough, one sneeze, or sore throat, there will be another.

Negativity is like a lingering virus with all its shared symptoms of discouragement, disagreeable attitudes, pessimism, hopelessness, and gloom. Negativity can spread undetectably from one person to another. Remember, it needs a host, another living human carrier. Once you come into contact with the host, you must be swift and discerning to avoid being infected yourself.

In 1 Thessalonians 5:22, the Apostle Paul speaks plainly to this matter: "Shun the very appearance of evil." As we say in our neighborhood, "Don't let 'Nobody' bring you down." Simply tell them, "Not Today." Then add, "This is the day that the Lord has made and I will REJOICE and BE GLAD in it" (Psalm 118:24).

The psalmist wrote those words from a place of distress & disparity. Have you ever had to bless God from a hard place, a place of adversity and pain?

Oh, but there is something about the name of Jesus that makes everything alright! Even in times of trouble, the psalmist writes with confidence that there is victory through the name of the Lord. The Lord, he says, is on my side, and therefore, I will not fear what anyone can do to me (v.6).

The word for you today is "adopt a positive attitude." With the psalmist, choose optimism, hope, and confidence. Jesus told us to be of good cheer (John 16:33). Allow the Lord to be your antidote to toxic situations. "The name of the Lord is a strong tower and the righteous run into it and are safe" (Proverbs 18:10). Embrace his words in Psalms 118 verse 17 in your moments of disparity: "That I shall live and not die, but I will declare the works of Lord."

Have great confidence as you put your trust in the Lord today and every day, for He is your strength, your song, and your salvation (v.14). Call upon the name of the Lord, and He will fight for you. 1 Thessalonians 5:16 invites us to "rejoice evermore!" Jesus has overcome the world and all the entrapments of the enemy. And so can you!

Now go. Spread the news. There's hope and victory over the plague of pessimism!

Chapter 16

Perseverance Is An Act of Will

Scripture: Philippians 2-8 NIV

Perseverance: grit, determination, persistence. This is not an unfamiliar word, but here at the start, let us take a closer look at what all this word really means.

The word perseverance has its origin in Middle English, so it has been around for a while. It's a noun that means "steadfastness in doing something despite difficulty or delay in achieving success." People with persistence accomplish tasks and meet their goals despite opposition, distractions, discouragement, and adversity. One that can persevere will rise to the occasion when faced with obstacles. They will find a way through, around, above, or under them. An individual with a mindset to conquer definitely will.

Perseverance reminds us of 1 Corinthians 15:58 can be a spiritual trait as well: "Therefore, my beloved brethren, be ye steadfast, unmovable, always abounding in the work of the Lord, forasmuch as ye know that your labour is not in vain in the Lord" (KJV). The act of the will is the ability to act with intent and purpose. I have a tee-shirt, for example, that reads "She Believed that She Could, So She Did." The message points clearly to an act of the will, but the seed of that will comes from "believed."

All steadfastness or perseverance has its roots in what we believe. Perseverance grounded in faith causes one to stay engaged even when they do not see immediate results, even when there seems to be no reciprocity. Those who persevere stay the course and endure to the end, even when it appears they are not changing anything.

To remain steadfast, our faith must be sure. And the scripture tells us that we are to "give thanks to God who has given us the victory through our Lord Jesus Christ" (1 Corinthians 15:57). In other words, look up. Our hope is not in the immediate results but in the call of Christ on our lives. Jesus kept going, even though He wept because of the people's unbelief.

I have seen the attendance at "The Reform" go up and down, but we persevere.

As Pastor Shawyrl R. Williams often says, "It takes a mind to do anything." The Word of God bears out her insight as it repeatedly addresses "the mind." Romans 12:2, for example, speaks of the "renewing of your mind." Truth is received in the mind and passed to the heart. As my heart receives it, that truth becomes a core conviction. And conviction is a driving force that transforms my life. In everything you do, you must have the appropriate mindset if you are going to work with all your heart.

But in Philippians 2:5, the Apostle Paul raises the bar: "have the same mindset as Christ Jesus." Many may read those words, but do they really understand that Paul is saying that our mind is to reflect the mind of Christ. The profound depth of those words requires us to look far beyond the surface.

This whole discussion about perseverance has focused on the will. The will is a product of a mind and heart focused on Jesus, whose mind was set on doing the will of God and completing God's purpose for His life. We know that God so loved us that He gave His Son (John 3:16), but we see the perseverance of Jesus in John 3:16, in which we read that Christ gave Himself to the Father's eternal purpose.

We also need to notice that Paul's words in Philippians 2:5 about having the same mind as Christ are preceded by a description of our frame of mind toward others in verses 2-4: Make my joy complete by being like-minded, having the same love, being one in spirit and of one mind. Do nothing out of selfish ambition or vain conceit. Rather, in humility, value others above yourselves, not looking to your own interests but each of you to the interests of the others (NIV).

Then he adds in verse 5, "In your relationships with one another, have the same mindset as Christ Jesus."

Notice that:

1. Our mindset is not only like His but comes from Him.
2. Our minds are comforted by love from God as well as one another.
3. We share a common bond in spirit with one another and with Christ
4. Our minds and hearts are characterized by tenderness, compassion, and like-mindedness. We share the same love with Christ we share commonly, and we are one in spirit and mind.

But Paul does not stop there. He takes us even deeper in the verses that follow. The mindset we are to share with Christ chooses to humble Himself, even take on a servant role (see verses 6-8).

Jesus persevered even through the agony of the cross. His heart and mind were set on completing God's plan. Jesus, who chose a servant's posture, was later "highly exalted and receiving a name which is above every name" (v. 9).

As we share His mind and heart and humble ourselves to serve others, we, too, will one day be rewarded for our perseverance in God's purpose for our lives.

Set your heart and mind to persevere. Turn to the One before whom every knee will bow and every tongue will confess that He is Lord. Let Him give you the heart and mind to persevere and fulfill His purpose.

Chapter 17

Rhema

Scripture: Deuteronomy 8:1-3 AMP

In Matthew 4, we read of Christ's temptation by the Devil. The enemy knew Jesus had been fasting for many days and was hungry, so he tempted Him to break His fast and eat something. Jesus replied that we don't live by natural food alone. If we want real, lasting life, we need "every word that comes out of the mouth of God" (Matthew 4:4).

God has spoken, and we have the written word. But God did not go silent. He continues to speak to those who have ears to hear.

We are talking about rhema, a Greek word that refers to something spoken. Specifically, we are talking about the voice of God who speaks to us if we will but listen.

In the truest sense, Rhema is the voice of God, quickening our understanding, prompting us to act on truth. The rhema comes to us through the Holy Spirit, who pours into our lives, sharing God's personal messages to us. A rhema word can also come by reading the Word of God, even a specific text. And it may come through a word that another has shared, and God then chooses to enlighten us personally.

When the rhema of God comes to us, truth comes alive. It may bring us hope and change, or we may find that a truth He has quickened within us helps change our present circumstances.

The rhema of God is always completely compatible with the Logos or written Word. God's word is infallible, meaning it is true without failure and will not return unto God void. The Bible is our guide to a righteous relationship with God. The logos and the added blessing of a rhema word have articulated who He is and His desires for us.

Second Timothy 3:16-17 speaks clearly to this:

All scripture is given by inspiration of God, and is profitable for doctrine, for reproof, for correction, for instruction in righteousness: That the man of God may be perfect, thoroughly furnished unto all good works.

Rhema brings us a fresh quickening from God to keep us on the right path and up close and personal with GOD. Knowing the Word of God helps us to resist the temptations and attacks by the adversary, but the Bible is our final word. We are to "study to shew thyself approved unto God, a workman that needeth not to be ashamed, rightly dividing the word of truth (2 Timothy 2:15, KJV).

In the opening paragraph, we noted the temptation Christ endured in which he was tempted to break His fast. The words He spoke were from Deuteronomy 8:1-3, in which we read that God had fed His people with manna while they were in the wilderness. Jesus was prompted by the Spirit of God there in His wilderness temptation to remember those words and apply them directly to His circumstances.

The key at that moment in Jesus' life, and in ours as well: know the Word of God. God's prompting wrote it to holy men, but by the rhema voice within us, that word becomes fresh and shines the light of truth into our days.

I believe that a rhema word for each reader may come from Ephesians 6:17 to take "the sword of the Spirit, which is the word of

God" as part of your spiritual armor. As God calls your attention to that verse, listen closely as He reminds you to cling to His word (logos) and be attentive to His rhema that provides us with fresh insight.

Chapter 18

We Must Persuade Them

Scripture: Psalms 19:14

"Let the words of my mouth, and the mediation of my heart, be acceptable in thy sight, O Lord, my strength and my redeemer."

David's prayer is often shared as a sincere petition by believers worldwide. But what motivated David to pray this way?

Let's look for a moment at verse 1: "The heavens declare the glory of God; and the firmament [skies] sheweth his handywork." And the following few verses paint an even more comprehensive picture:

Day unto day uttereth speech, and night unto night sheweth knowledge. There is no speech nor language, where their voice is not heard. Their line is gone out through all the earth, and their words to the end of the world (v. 2-4a).

On one occasion, when the multitude was shouting praises to Jesus, the Pharisees objected. Jesus then replied, "I tell you that, if these should hold their peace, the stones would immediately cry out" (Luke 19:40, NIV).

In another place, the Apostle Paul boldly announced:

The wrath of God is being revealed from heaven against all the godlessness and wickedness of people, who suppress the truth by their wickedness, since what may be known about God is plain to them, because God has made it plain to them. For since the creation of the world, God's invisible qualities—his eternal power and divine nature—have been clearly seen, being understood from what has been made, so that people are without excuse (Romans 1:18-20, NIV).

When they realize that God exists, they also become aware that they need to seek Him. But later in Romans 10:14, Paul returns to this subject:

How then shall they call on him in whom they have not believed? And how shall they believe in him of whom they have not heard?

At the end of the verse, he is straightforward when he asks how people can hear if no one tells them.

If creation declares who God is, one must ask, what about us? We are the crowning glory of His creation. So surely our declaration of God should shine with His glory even more brightly and clearly than any other part of His creation.

I believe our mandate is to let our light shine with His presence through us and persuade them to seek Him and discover His grace.

What, then, do we need to do?

Let us start with the words of David in Psalm 19:14: "Let the words of my mouth, and the mediation of my heart, be acceptable in thy sight, O Lord, my strength and my redeemer." As we encounter others, our words and our hearts should glow with His countenance, making it clear that He is our Redeemer and the source of our strength.

Timothy calls us to study, deliberately, and purposefully grow in our understanding of scripture. Then, as we learn from God's voice to us in the scriptures, His smile of approval will rest on us. We will be equipped to "rightly divide the truth" so that we won't experience the shame of misleading someone (see 1 Timothy 2:15).

As good sharers, we must also seek wisdom and understanding (Proverbs 1:4). Solomon is not talking about having an extremely good sense or insight because what we seek is the One who is Wisdom. Our seeking comes through our personal growth as we walk with Him and the blessing of His rhema.

It is also important to note that Solomon speaks of Wisdom using the pronoun "she." Do not be misled by this. This is still referring to God. Christ once referred to Himself as a mother hen who lovingly protects her peeps. The feminine reference to God here is describing something about Him that we might not fully discover otherwise. He is pointing out His nurturing nature. The part of His nature is usually not depicted by a masculine image. Men can be nurturing, but God has placed an added special instinct in a woman that blesses her with an extra measure of a nurturing nature. God made both male and female in His likeness, so God chooses here to reveal a part of Him that is generally more evident in the woman. He wants us to discover the true depth of His nurturing nature.

The call to persuade others and the nurturing nature are woven into the single fabric of our ministry tasks. Since it is not our lives but Christ's life living through us, His heart to persuade and nurture will be evidenced to those around us.

Chapter 19

Level Up

Scripture: John 15: 1-12 AMP

Recently God gave me a revelation to share with His people about keeping our focus. And sometimes that is difficult.

We belong to two worlds.

As citizens of God's Kingdom, we seek His righteousness. We desire to please the Lord and reflect His grace. But we live in this world with so much that distracts us from righteousness and grace. The idols in this life are many: money, success, the lure of pleasure, and the call of righteousness require us to set such things aside. Rather than allowing the temporal things around us to dominate our minds, we must set our minds and hearts on God's Kingdom. We must focus on those good things that come from above (James 1:17), eternal things, rather than things that will pass away.

That is why "we as believers must self-evaluate our level of relationship. If we truly love God, the question then is, 'Would God be pleased?'" (Minister Clarysa Philpot). So then, with eyes fixed on His glory, we must look at our place in God's Kingdom the same way the eye of the eagle zeros in on the prize it seeks to nourish and sustain it.

And so, in this time of change and challenge, my message I

brought to the church was: Don't "do you" in this season. "Do God." Put another way, don't be so focused on yourself and your agenda that a focus on God's desires and plans are set aside on some dusty shelf of your life. Our call to righteous living requires us to keep our focus in the right direction.

I have often been reminded of the song lyrics "Is God Satisfied with me?" Is He satisfied with the way I walk? Is He satisfied with the way I talk? Is He satisfied with my life? If He is satisfied, then everything is alright.

No one can answer that question for you. This is an individual issue, a self-evaluation. In writing to the church of Corinth, Paul says, "Examine yourselves, whether ye be in the faith; prove your own selves. Know ye not your own selves, how that Jesus Christ is in you, except ye be reprobates? (2 Corinthians 13:5,   KJV) The Apostle is challenging them to conduct "spiritual checkups   ," just as you schedule your annual physical checkup. We naturally love to tell others about a good doctor's report. "My blood pressure was good, like a kid," etc. But, how much more important is a spiritual checkup to determine if we are bearing the fruit of Jesus Christ or if we are counterfeits. We all must have the spiritual DNA of Jesus Christ. When the trumpet sounds, no flesh shall enter in.

While our spiritual examinations require us to be honest with ourselves, we must invite the Spirit of God to be in charge. He will help us see clearly as we review the fruits of the Spirit in Galatians 5:22-23 to evaluate our spiritual health:

1. Love
2. Joy
3. Peace
4. Longsuffering (patience)
5. Gentleness
6. Goodness
7. Faith
8. Meekness

9. Temperance (self-control)

Bearing much fruit allows God to be glorified. Remember, He inhabits the praises of His people!

Let me add that if you are striving for a good report, stay connected to the Vine. Let His righteousness flow through you. By His Spirit, He will let His likeness flow through you. He does not just love, but He is Love; and His Spirit will infuse us with that love, unconditional Agape love.

This is my commandment, that you love one another, as I have loved you! John 15:12, NIV

Level up, Branches.

Be Infectious!

Chapter 20

Know Your Worth (Part 1)
Scripture: Psalms 8:1-9 NIV

Proverbs helps us to understand that the "fear of the LORD is the beginning of wisdom: and the knowledge of the holy is understanding" (Proverbs 9:10). Regardless of how much education we may get or how much life experience we gain, it is only when we enter into a relationship with a holy God that we truly gain wisdom and understanding.

What better teacher of life than the Creator of life helping us discover the awe of living with wisdom and understanding. Many spend years searching to fill a void in their lives. Yet as much as they yearn to learn and find answers, they often do not know where to find them. Some may stay in the chase. Others may fall by the wayside into lives of complacency and never rise to their full potential. And so, very many find themselves under a cloud of pessimism. Those who strive to gain knowledge, as well as those who stall out, can easily find themselves living under a cloud of pessimism and the hopelessness that fills their minds with the gloom of settling for "this is just the way I am."

I beg you, never become comfortable with that state of mind. Instead, seek the One in whom wisdom dwells and who is indeed

Wisdom Himself. Only through Him can you discover that your worth is in who He has shaped you to be. Find the comfort of seeing yourself as the person He planned for you to become.

It is imperative in this season that we learn who we are in God's eyes and how valuable we are to Him. Genesis 1:26-27 declares that we were "created in His image and likeliness." He sees His own image when he looks at us, and He longs for us to reflect Him and His nature to others.

Only those who through Wisdom have become aware of who they are and how much they are worth can truly declare with the psalmist, "O Lord our Lord, how excellent is thy name in all the earth! who hast set thy glory in the heavens" (Psalm 8:1, KJV).

David is intrigued with his value to God. So, in Psalm 8:4 (KJV), he poses the question, "What is man, that thou art mindful of him? and the son man, that thou visitest him?"

For many years, like David, generations have struggled to find their value. But unfortunately, this inner struggle has caused many to miss some profound opportunities and milestones of grace across their life spans.

Please discover who God sees you as and how much you are worth to Him today.

Chapter 21

Know Your Worth (Part 2)

Scripture: Psalms 8:1-9 NIV

Humility. Self-deprecation.

As different as these two terms are, they are often confused. Even when people define them differently, they too easily view themselves through the wrong lens.

The scriptures often admonish us to be humble:

Humble yourselves before the Lord (James 4:10).
Be humble and gentle (Ephesians 4:2).
In humility, value others above yourselves (Philippians 2:3).
With humility comes wisdom (Proverbs 11:2).

The humility that God wants us to have comes from proper respect for the way God Himself sees us. God looked at His creation, including us, and declared it was "good." So, true humility never includes devaluing ourselves but rather gladly acknowledging that we are made to shine with His likeness. Therefore, every expression of humility in the verses above starts with a proper perspective of our relationship as the created with the Creator.

Self-deprecation, on the other hand, starts at the wrong place.

When our eyes are fixed on ourselves, our sense of our own value becomes twisted. We either tend to "think too highly of ourselves" (Proverbs 3:7), or we easily swing the other direction and depreciate ourselves. Instead of seeing our value as God intended, we become critical of ourselves, devaluing our worth, missing God's plan for us. Such a misdirected perspective will only thwart and stagnate you from moving forward with your life.

True humility lifts you and will take you a long way in God's purpose for you. So, in Psalm 8, we hear David's prayer of humility expressed in thankfulness:

For thou hast made him a little lower than the angels, and hast crowned him with glory and honour. God gave mankind dominion over the works of His hands and put all things under his feet (v. 5-6, KJV).

I like to make that personal: "under my feet." This is not an expression of pride but genuine humility.

With such great authority, there is great responsibility and accountability. This is a position of stewardship. For he is monitoring your stewardship, and if you are faithful over a few things, God will make you ruler over more (Matthew 25:21).

The next time you question your worth or are down on yourself and feeling insignificant, show the enemy who you are. The enemy is a bully, so rise up and remind him that God made you a little lower than the angels. When it is said and done, He will crown you with glory and honor because You march under His banner, His authority. You bear His Seal. You meet His approval.

Declare with David in Psalm 8:9, "O Lord our Lord, how excellent is thy name in all the earth!" as a reminder to yourself as well as the enemy how valuable you are to Him. (v. 8-9, KJV)

One added thought: choose at least five positive words that describe your worth in God's eyes. Write them down. Keep them handy.

And encourage someone else to discover their worth!

Chapter 22

I Need My "Jump"

Scripture: Luke 1:37, 41 KJV

In a casual conversation, I heard "Evangelist Elect" Carmen Manual in my church say something I will remember for a long time.

In reference to a car jump, she prodded, "Is the power behind the jump?" The question has never left my mind.

Was this a word I was to preach or hold on to for some point in time? I pondered her words and what I heard in my heart. Is there power in my "jump?" So here it is Tuesday 12:33 a.m., and God has me typing "The Word for Today: I Need My Jump."

I need my boost of power, if you will. First, I need to be sure I am leaping in the right direction. Then, I need to be recharged to regain my surge, encouragement, and reassurance!

From her conversation, I have gained a fresh understanding that our "jump" should not be taken lightly but approached with thankfulness.

There is always a risk with every leap we take. Not everything we try to do goes the way we expect it. Regardless of the outcome, each leap becomes a time to learn from God how to move forward.

Nothing we experience should be seen as a waste of time. Don't let go of what you were trying to do until you sense that God is telling you to move forward in a different direction. Always find value in what you attempt. Build on it. Learn and grow from it. Gain wisdom as you reflect on the experience. Grow in your faith in God's power.

In Luke chapter 1, we discover Elizabeth, the cousin of Mary, experiencing her own leap. She became pregnant with John, who would become a great evangelist pointing the nation to Jesus. This formerly barren woman was faced with a major "jump." The angel Gabriel had been sent from God in verses 13-15, telling Zacharias and his wife Elizabeth that she would bring forth a son, and his name was to be John. They were told to have joy and rejoice with gladness, for he was to be "great in the sight of the Lord." And they were told that he would be filled with the Holy Ghost, even in his mother's womb.

Elizabeth had yet another "jump" when her cousin showed up. But this time, it was her baby who, the scripture says, "leaped" within her with a supernatural awareness of the presence of Mary's baby boy, who was the Savior of the world.

Elizabeth recognized her experience for what it was and broke into a song of praise when Mary arrived: "as soon as the voice of thy salutation sounded in mine ears, the babe leaped in my womb for joy." Being filled with the Holy Ghost, Elizabeth was filled with great joy. This woman of God was to bear a son who would be "the voice crying in the wilderness" for the people of Israel to be ready. The Savior was coming.

God called Elizabeth to experience her own leap of faith.

We have all heard it said that God may not come when we want Him to come, but He comes in His own time. It is also true that He may not come the way we thought He would, but He is faithful to come as He promised.

God, help us become sensitive to His Spirit and recognize, appreciate, and value those times in our lives when we are called on to take a leap in our walk of faith.

At times, God may appoint us to a "jump" that calls us to encourage and be a supporter of others taking their leap in faith. Our role may be to share the challenge of another and enable them, as Elizabeth did for Mary, to rejoice and magnify the Lord.

Chapter 23

It Only Takes Two

Scripture: Matthew 18:19-20

Life is a journey, an experience that should be lived out intentionally, purpose-driven, motivated, and guided divinely.

For Christians, the Word of God unlocks that sense of purpose. Its pages are filled with the history of God at work in this world, a history that reveals salvation and eternal life. It is filled with examples, mysteries, parables, and captivating songs of conviction, help, and deliverance.

This inspired record of God's hand in our history has transcended generations. And it is still potent, transforming the lives of all who hear and treasure its message of grace in their hearts, those who "hide the word" in their hearts, so they will not "sin against God" (Psalm 119:11).

Before declaring his commitment to hiding God's word in his heart, the writer of this unusual poem posed an important question in verse 9: How can a young person stay on the path of purity? Living in a land of impurity, how can he stay on course and not fall by the wayside? He answers the question quite simply: "By living according to [God's] word."

The commitment in verse 11 to value God's word was the solution to his earlier question about living a pure life. The answer to all of life's questions can be found in the Word of God. The poet is determined not to wander away from the commandments of God. He knows that those who love God take heed to His word.

While some long to follow God, there are others whose purpose is to plot ways to lure the seeker away. We will encounter the adversary who lurks and devises ways to distract our hearts and minds on this journey of grace and faith. And it is not unusual that the most common detractor can be close to us, particularly those whose lifestyles are appealing.

There is an old saying that one rotten apple can spoil the whole bunch. In Numbers 13 and 14, we see 12 spies from Israel were sent to assess the new land and note what they could expect when they tried to take it over. Of the 12, only Joshua and Caleb came back with good reports. The other 10 created doubt in everyone's mind and tried to convince people that it would be dangerous.

Like the Israelites who had come so far, many fail to take possession of what has been promised to them.

On our journey, we have a decision to make. We can listen to the ten full of fear or the two filled with faith. Be wise and peg those who seek to detour you, then put a distance between them and yourself.

Remember, it only takes two! Matthew 18:19-20 declares that "if two of you shall agree on earth as touching anything they shall ask, it shall be done for them of my Father which is in heaven. For where two or three are gathered together in my name, there am I in the midst of them."

Chapter 24

Forever Changed

Scripture: Acts 9:1-4, 17 (KJV)

Tamala Mann has a new rendition of the song "Change," in which she sings,

"Wonderful change has come over me" and "I'm so glad He changed me."

The song speaks of this change as a wonderful experience. It evokes the listeners to reflect deeply on the effect of the change that has come over them. It resonates with our spirits and causes us to rise to our feet, lift our hands and sing the words of gratefulness for the difference in our lives. Whether that change was planned or unplanned, we can be thankful that God has lovingly made a difference in us.

Just pause, and for a moment, journey back, letting the images fan freely.

Give way to the waves of praise and gratitude that swell up within you. Identify the changes. Identify what God has brought you through and from what you have been set free.

Meditate often on Paul's declaration: "Therefore if any man be in

Christ he is a new creature: old things are passed away; behold, all things are become new (2 Corinthians 5:17, KJV).

When Jesus was talking with Nicodemus, He called this being "born again." What an amazing picture! Nicodemus, of course, did not understand, and he asked, "How can a man be born when he is old? Can he enter the second time into his mother's womb?"

Jesus answered him, "Except a man be born of the water and of the spirit, he cannot see the Kingdom of God" (See John 3:3-5, KJV). The change Jesus is describing is radical and wonderful at the same time. Those who have experienced such a dramatic change must purpose to never return to the life they have left behind.

A man named Saul experienced this kind of life-altering change. On his way to Damascus, this Pharisee, who was commissioned to imprison Christians, was confronted by Christ Himself. Knocked off his high horse and faced with the thunderous voice of Christ, Saul was brought to his knees and blinded for three days.

This was God's version of "scared straight."

But God did not leave him alone. Under direct orders from God, a devout Christian named Ananias went to the house where Saul was staying and praying. The scripture tells us:

> "Ananias...entered into the house; and putting his hands on him said, 'Brother Saul, the Lord, even Jesus, that appeared unto thee in the way as thou camest, hath sent me, that thou mightest receive thy sight, and be filled with the Holy Ghost.' And immediately there fell from his eyes as it had been scales: and he received sight forthwith, and arose, and was baptized."

Notice that Saul was not the only one who was changed that day. Ananias knew who Saul was and what he intended to do. Still, Ananias was changed when God told him what he was to do, and to minister to this persecutor, Ananias had to take God at His word.

But Saul's change was not complete yet. Saul's whole identity changed. This persecutor emerged as the great evangelist Paul. Paul immediately embraced and lived out his transformation. Beginning in the synagogue, Paul traveled throughout the Gentile world, declaring the Lordship of Christ. Acts 9:22 tells us that Paul's new identity and message confounded the Jews, who had only known him as their enemy.

Seek God to truly change your life, to make you a whole new person. And never turn again to who you used to be.

Chapter 25

Allow The Good News That You Know About Christ To Affect Your Life

Scripture: Hebrews 4:12

In our discussion of "change," we must take care to be receptive to the transformational work of God. God is ready to change us, but for the good news about Christ to have a lasting effect in your life, we must allow it.

The scriptures reveal that the Hebrews failed to allow God to transform them fully. Numbers 13 and 14 remind us that an entire generation of Israel's nation could not see their promised land because they had lost their faith. Instead, they lived in unbelief and disobedience. In Hebrews 4:2, we read, "For unto us was the gospel preached, as well as unto them: but the word preached did not profit them, not being mixed with faith in them that heard it."

There is only one Author of life, physical or spiritual, and that is God Creator, who is at work through His son Jesus. John records the familiar words "in the beginning was the Word and the Word was with God and the Word was God" (John 1:1). He goes on in verses 3 and 4 to declare, "All things were made by him; and without him was not anything made that was made. In him was life; and the life was the light of men."

The Word in John's text refers to Jesus. That Word was present and actively a part of creation. He is the Living Word in whom all life has its origin. And this Author of life is the Source of our new life as well. Apart from Him, we have no life at all.

The writer of Hebrews points out that the only way to experience this life is by faith, because "without faith it is impossible to please him: for he that comes to God must believe that he is and that he is a rewarder of them that diligently seek him" (Hebrews 11:6). Therefore, if we are to experience new life and continue to live in Christ, we need to maintain our life of faith. This message of faith must continue to resonate every day. If we choose to turn back and fall away from the faith, we no longer are alive in Christ. There is no other source of life apart from Him.

The psalmist David in Psalms 95:7-8 invites us to recognize God as our God and see ourselves as the people of his pasture and the sheep of his hand. So today, if we truly hear his voice. "harden not your heart, as in the provocation [rebellion], and as in the day of the temptation in the wilderness (bracketed text inserted).

We know from Exodus 17:7 that Israel chided and tempted the Lord, saying, "Is the Lord amongst us or not?" Hebrews 4:11 speaks of the "rest" available in God, a rest that calls up the image of the promised land Israel was forbidden to enter because of their unbelief. Yet God has a rest for us, a spiritual promised land of eternal life for us as we remain faithful to Him. In 17:11, we are admonished to "labour therefore to enter into that rest, lest any man fall after the same example of unbelief [referring back to verse 7].

Let us fight on(!), laying aside any weight that might hinder us. We must not let the cares of this world interfere with our faith but allow the living word of God to have the full range in our lives. For the word of God is quick, living, powerful, and "sharper than any two-edged sword" (Hebrews 4:12). His word pierces even to the "dividing asunder of soul and spirit," showing us who we are and who we are not, discerning and revealing the thoughts and intents of our hearts, even the core of our moral and spiritual lives.

Allow the good news of life in Christ to affect your life and guide you to the reality of rest in Him!

Chapter 26

How To Declare A Thing
Scripture: Job 22:28 KJV

Declare and Decree are very powerful words.

To declare is to state clearly or make known, to proclaim, to communicate. People make all kinds of statements or declarations, but not everybody can back up what they say. A declaration that has meaning has fact and evidence to verify it.

A decree is a decision or a judgment, or as Webster states, "a formal and authoritative order." A decree is also a "command, commandment, mandate, or rule." Behind a decree must be a recognized authority.

Understanding the definitions of both words helps us discover how they apply to our lives.

For a moment, let us turn our attention to the account of Job. The overall picture of this book is the stark image of a man experiencing great suffering at Satan's hands. His suffering was so great that we are told he lost everything he had in this world, including, in the end, even his family.

Yet in Job 1:1, we are introduced to this man from the land of Uz, as perfect, upright, one that feared God and shunned (or eschewed) evil.

However, by the time we get to Job 22, we find a disturbing conversation. The speaker is one of Job's "comforters," Eliphaz the Temanite. Like the others who had come to "comfort" Job, Eliphaz had concluded that Job had sinned (probably greatly) and God was punishing him.

According to Eliphaz, Job is pious. He must have become proud of it, so God is displeased with him. He goes on to assume Job has been a horrendous sinner; he must have lent money to someone and then demanded it is paid back with so much interest that he stripped the poor guy clean to the bone, or he may have even been so full of evil that he had mistreated widows and orphans.

Eliphaz then calls on Job to turn to God with a repentant heart:

"Acquaint [or re-acquaint] now thyself with him, and be at peace: thereby good shall come unto thee. Receive, I pray thee, the law from his mouth, and lay up his words in thine heart. If thou return to the Almighty, thou shalt be built up, thou shalt put away iniquity far from thy tabernacles... Yea, the Almighty shall be thy defense" (Job 22:21-23, 25; bracket text implied).

And then Eliphaz notes encouragingly that with a repentant heart, if "thou shalt make thy prayer unto him, and he shall hear thee, and thou shalt pay thy vows.... (And at this point we find the word decree as Eliphaz continues adding, if you repent, "thou shalt also decree a thing, and it shall be established unto thee: and the light shall shine [once again] upon thy ways" (Job 22:27-28), the bracketed text is implied in this context).

This whole account reveals an important truth. If we live in a way that honors God, we can decree what is in keeping with God's heart, and it will be honored by Him. But, on the other hand, if we are not living a life pleasing to God, our decree has no authority behind it.

Have you ever found yourself facing tough times? Have you felt the pain of loss?

Perhaps others around you have questioned whether God is showing His displeasure with you. Or maybe you have examined your own life and asked that same question.

If you recognize that you need to repent of some failure or sin in your life, then do not delay. Instead, turn to God, who loves you. Even if you are not aware of any sin, follow Job's example in 7:20-21, 9:20, 13:23 and profess your desire to be transparent before Him, express your sorrow if there have been failures in your life that have displeased Him, then declare Him to be Lord of your life.

The key in this matter is to submit to His authority and grace. Then, in His own time, the evidence of His favor will return, and you will confidently be able to decree truths that come from His heart and thus have fruit in your life.

Chapter 27

Loving God, Loving Others

Scripture: Matthew 22:37-39 (KJV)

How do you measure up?

In Christ, we are worthy!

When I recently spoke about being worthy, I emphasized that once I have repented, confessed with my mouth, believed in my heart, I must continue to live a life that seeks to know the Savior more and more. That means that I must seek to be filled with the Spirit of God.

Walking a life that is responsive to the prodding and nudging of the Holy Spirit makes it possible for me to know God more intimately. It assures me that I am in a right relationship with Him through the love of Christ in whom I live and who lives in me.

Our position of grace with Christ does not come from anything we have done. Our righteousness is from Him alone. We have none of our own. We are saved by grace, not by works that would allow us to boast. Instead, all our boasting is centered on Him. Jesus is the One who changed the trajectory of our lives and brought us into the right relationship with God.

Paul truly understood the wonder of such grace. He sought to know Christ above all else:

"I consider everything else in life for loss because of the surpassing worth of knowing Christ Jesus my Lord, for whose sake I have lost all things. I consider them garbage, that I may gain Christ and be found in him, not having a righteousness of my own that comes from the law, but that which is through faith in Christ the righteousness that comes from God on the basis of faith. I want to know Christ – yes to know the power of his resurrection, and to participate in his sufferings, becoming like him in his death" (Philippians 3:8-10, NIV).

This was Paul's highest calling, one he pursued with deep conviction, so deep that Paul spoke of himself as a "slave" to the Gospel of Christ (Romans 1:1). Paul gave up things that may have been pleasurable in his relationship with Christ so that his life and service would give pleasure to Christ. At the heart of this relationship is a deep and motivating love.

God loved us so much that He gave His Son (John 3:16), and the Son loves us so much that He willingly gave Himself to be our Savior (1 John 3:16). The motivation to provide us with salvation at such a high price was a deep and eternal love.

This kind of love is called agape love. Agape love is unconditional, unwavering, and has nothing to do with what we deserve or anything we could ever do to deserve it. Instead, it inhabits a forgiving, holy, righteous, and never-changing God. When He declares His love, we never need to doubt Him. He cannot lie since He is Truth. And the foundation of our relationship with Him is His everlasting love for those who have been created in His image.

On our part, we seek Him only. There is no other Source of grace. He alone is God. He is protectively jealous, lovingly possessive, and there is no other God except Him. Those of us who ardently seek Him do so because we know there is no other. He alone embodies "love so amazing, so divine (lyrics of When I Survey the Wondrous Cross) that as those who bear His image, we find no other worthy of our love.

There are many gods, all the product of sinful hearts and wicked imaginations. Israel lost sight of God because their wayward hearts were drawn to worldly desires. They sought to manipulate the very idols they had come to embrace. God reminded them that He alone was God, and despite their sinful waywardness, He alone loved them.

To love Him and to accept His love is our highest calling.

One day a Pharisee, a lawyer or expert in Mosaic law, asked Jesus, "Master, which is the great commandment in the law?" Jesus said unto him, "Thou shalt love the Lord thy God with all thy heart, and with all thy soul, and with all thy mind. This is the first and great commandment."

Then without taking a breath, Jesus added, "And the second is like unto it, 'Thou shalt love thy neighbor as thyself'" (Matthew 22:36-39. KJV).

Christ redefined our love for Him as a love that we extend to others with those words.

This is a powerful statement. The command to love God is to manifest in our love for others. Our love for others is to be the same love we have for Him since He alone is Love. He is the reason we have the capacity to love at all.

We can only love Him because the Spirit draws us to Him and fills us with His love first. And we are then called to love others with His love. That includes our neighbors and our enemies as well, and we are to love them as much as we love ourselves.

Only as we experience Love that changes us into His likeness can we know love at all.

What do you want in your life? What is the deepest convicting urge that motivates your life? As God's children, we must allow nothing but the blood of Jesus poured out through His love to define our hopes and, indeed, even ourselves.

Chapter 28

"Hind" Strength

Scripture: Psalms 18:32-33 KJV

Life presents some very challenging situations; some greater, some smaller.

In one sense, each challenge is unique to each person; yet we all encounter the same kinds of tests and tasks. For example, Hebrews 4:15 reveals that even Jesus faced temptations, and as the writer goes on to make clear, He was tempted in every way the rest of us are.

As common as our temptations and tests and ordeals in life may be, each has a uniqueness. After all, we are individuals, and each challenge produces a uniquely personal reaction.

Regardless of how unique or shared, they may be, our challenges come from two sources. Either they are visited on us at the hands of another, or some we may have brought upon ourselves. But to be clear, life certainly presents some very challenging situations.

So how do we face such times?

Many face them alone. They may have friends to sympathize with them, but they can provide only limited help. Yet we are told to "be strong and of a good courage; be not afraid, neither be thou dismayed: for the LORD thy God is with thee whithersoever thou goest." Let that sink in. He is not only aware of each test we face, but He is with us and stays at our side.

In Psalm 18:18-19, David proclaims that "the LORD was my support. He brought me out into a spacious place. He rescued me because He delighted in me". And David had ample experience to make such a declaration. God had delivered him from the hands of Saul and his enemies.

Because God had proven himself to David, David breaks out in his poetic voice with songs of praise, testifying to the many ways God has rescued him. Throughout the psalms, David declares that God is his Lord, his Strength, his Rock. He calls Him his Fortress, His Deliverer, Buckler, his personal Horn of Salvation, and High Tower. No wonder David confesses his confidence in God: "I will call upon the name of the Lord, who is worthy to be praised. Because I call upon the name of the Lord I shall be saved from my enemies (Psalm 18:3. NIV).

David truly realizes the real source of his strength. In verses 32 and 33, he describes God as fortifying him with strength. "It is God that girdeth me with strength, and maketh my way perfect." David adds Not only does God ARM us with his strength he, "Keeps our way secure and sure as the hind's feet." The hind is a deer, one of the most secure animals in the world.

Listen to David's praise in verses 33-36:

He makes my feet like the feet of a deer; he causes me to stand on the heights. He trains my hands for battle; my arms can bend a bow of bronze. You make your saving help my shield, and your right hand sustains me; your help has made me great. You provide a broad path for my feet so that my ankles do not give way (NIV).

Strength, agility, a firm posture: God enables us to stand firm even when facing the tough and uncertain terrain of difficult times. He invites us to "stand [firmly and securely] and see the Salvation of the Lord" (Exodus 14:13).

To those who must face the ordeals of life, remember that God has promised to increase your strength (Isaiah 40:29). "They that wait upon the Lord shall renew their strength; they shall mount up with wings as eagles; they shall run and not weary; and they shall walk and not faint (Isaiah 40:31).

To echo the heart of David, let us declare: "I will call upon the name of the Lord who is worthy to be praised" (Psalm 18:3).

Chapter 29

Active Participation, Blessed Connected

Scripture: Psalms 34:5-6 KJV

The Blessing Connection

Many are still riding or living off the prayers of their mother, father, grandmother, grandfather, aunties, uncles, and or other family members. Only when we truly enter into our own relationship with God do we enter the true faith and actively participate in the blessing of His grace.

"Actively participate" implies an active partnership. In our relationship with God, we enjoy a special bond with Him that includes a reciprocal connection. What is shared is the awe and wonder of interdependence.

In biology, there is a special term that applies here: homeostasis. It means a capacity toward a relatively stable equilibrium or balance between interdependent elements. In biological science, this refers to physiological relationships; but in this case, we are focusing on a spiritual bond that allows us to experience a divinely planned balance. When we consider that we are created, and God is the Creator, we recognize that His abilities are far beyond our own. Yet, the equilibrium in this case still applies because the relationship has been divinely designed with God fully fulfilling His role. Each of us acting with all our inner beings to fill the place we were created to fill in this relationship.

This is the compatibility of commitment. If we are to have a stable relationship with Him, we are responsible for our faithfulness to be what God created us to be, just as God has chosen to declare His faithfulness to us.

Proverbs 9:10 has something critically important to this discussion: "The fear of the Lord is the beginning of wisdom: and the knowledge of the holy is understanding." Of course, the word fear may confuse people today because its meaning has changed over time. Nevertheless, the "knowledge of the holy" is an awesome thing. That experience causes us to see ourselves in contrast to God.

Isaiah 6:1-5 gives us a glimpse of this prophet's encounter with the presence of God.

In the year that King Uzziah died, I saw the Lord, high and exalted, seated on a throne; and the train of his robe filled the temple. Above him were seraphim, each with six wings: With two wings they covered their faces, with two they covered their feet, and with two they were flying. And they were calling to one another: "Holy, holy, holy is the LORD Almighty; the whole earth is full of his glory." At the sound of their voices, the doorposts and thresholds shook, and the temple was filled with smoke. "Woe to me!" I cried. "I am ruined! For I am a man of unclean lips, and I live among a people of unclean lips, and my eyes have seen the King, the LORD Almighty."

This is a holy fear, a reaction of awe mixed with the disparaging contrast between God's holiness and the feebleness of this devout and God-seeking prophet at his best.

It may seem like this example does not fit our discussion of a balanced relationship, but that is not the case. Remember, God fills His role with His eternal nature, and we respond with the uniqueness He has designed us to have. Our relationship grows through the discipline, instruction, and wisdom we receive from His generosity. We move further from the influence of our wicked world and abandon any wicked tendency within us just as ardently as God's holiness and grace draws us to Him.

Yet as imperfect human beings, we are humbled and recognize how needy and honored we are to enjoy the blessing of this relationship. The psalmist declared, "the angel of the Lord encamps around those who fear him" (Psalm 34:7), and in verse 9, "those who are filled with such awe will lack nothing."

This awareness, this holy awe, was evident in the way David lived his life. His psalms are filled with honor and praise, acknowledging God's part in this relationship, along with many expressions of his love and desire to please God and walk with Him. We can see even in David's failures that He sought to maintain his part of this special bond with God because David would fall on his knees in deep, even bitter repentance, calling on God to restore him to the place he enjoyed with God.

Our commitment to our relationships will be evident in our conduct as we walk with God. Our hearts will react to His presence with humility and an attitude of gratitude for His grace. Conversely, when we fall, we are grieved that we have caused Him grief and have failed to show His grace to others.

We are to actively be engaged in this relationship, not in perfect behavior but in the persistent conduct of humility and dependence on God.

When we are new believers, our relationship with God will afford us time to grow in Him. At first, we will need to learn to trust in tough times. Then, as we walk with Him, we experience His love, strength, and faithfulness. Repeatedly we will hear his invitation to "taste and see" that He is good. As we choose to be a part of God's plan for us to know Him, we are more and more filled with the awe of knowing Him rather than merely knowing about Him.

Let's take a look at Psalm 34 to see some of the ways we can actively participate in this process of discovering Him.

1. We are to seek the Lord: I sought the Lord, and he heard me; he delivered me from all my fears (v. 4).
2. We call out to Him: This poor man called, and the LORD heard him; he saved him out of all his troubles (v. 6 and 17).
3. We choose good over evil: Turn from evil and do good (v 14).
4. We choose peace: seek peace and pursue it (v. 14).

In verse 15, we read that "the eyes of the LORD are on the righteous, and his ears are attentive to their cry." If we are to experience the wonder and joy of living in connection with God, we must commit to being a part of the process, participants in this holy bond. At the heart of our part is our readiness to cry out in humility to God. He assures us that He is listening. Thus, not only do we sustain our relationship with Him, but we grow as well in His likeness, just as He planned.

So, cry out to Him. Turn to Him for his help. Ask and you will receive. Seek and you will find (Matthew 7:7).

Chapter 30

God's Grace and Mercy Makes Me Worthy

Scripture: Matthew 5:7

The words grace and mercy are often used together. However, when we look at them closely, we find that they are complementary.

Grace refers to unmerited or unearned favor. While we can exercise grace toward others, our version of this act pales against the completeness and measure of God's grace. Some say that grace is synonymous with love, so they speak of love unmerited as well. And while there is a natural connection, grace and love are not interchangeable. We can, however, speak of grace as unearned or unmerited love.

Love is a part of God's very nature. He, in fact, is love. But, on the other hand, Grace is the ultimate expression of His nature and is the product of His love.

Mercy, like grace, is bestowed on someone who does not deserve it or has not earned it; but mercy is a word related to judgment or penalty. To show mercy is to choose not to punish someone who deserves to be punished.

Often the two are described this way: grace is favor received though unearned, while mercy is favor to withhold the judgment that has been earned. In grace, we receive what we do not deserve. In mercy, we do not receive what we do deserve.

God sees us and knows us better than we know ourselves. His knowledge of us is complete. What motivates God is that He sees us as His created beings - created in His image and for His fellowship with Him, but who have strayed from His love. Yet as one songwriter has put it, "He looked beyond my fault and saw my need." The love of Jehovah God saw that we were wretched and undone, and in His grace took on the flesh of mankind and at the cross took on Himself our sins and unrighteousness; in His mercy, we were set free from the penalty of our sins.

So, what does it mean when someone says they have become worthy of God's goodness and favor? Let's be clear. Nothing we can ever do can make us worthy or deserving of His grace or His mercy. Yet, they are counted or made worthy for any who have received grace and mercy. Now, God looks at us and sees only the grace that covers us and declares that, in His Son, we are called worthy. This is the farthest or highest measure of God's grace and mercy.

The grace and mercy that He extends to us is the same grace and mercy that we must be willing to extend to others. Jesus told us in Matthew 18 about a servant who had been forgiven (an expression of both grace and mercy) yet failed to pass that same forgiveness to others. Yet we are clearly instructed in Ephesians 4:32 to "be kind and compassionate to one another, forgiving each other, just as in Christ God forgave you."

The Spirit of God who lives in us longs for us to be the vessels through which Christ's likeness is displayed to others. When Jesus modeled prayer for His disciples, He included these words: "forgive us our trespasses, as we forgive those who trespass against us" (Matthew 6:12, traditional wording). To live in a state of unforgiveness toward others will eventually disqualify us for God's forgiveness.

Christ told us "Blessed" are the merciful, for they shall receive Mercy. Simply remember the mercy bestowed unto you even when you were not worthy! And that "Behavior has Consequences." As Paul tells us in Galatians 6:7, "You reap what you Sow."- In God's Mercy, He tells us how to be Blessed in Him and to Be Happy in Doing So!

Of course, we know that we have been blessed by mercy being extended to us. But Jesus is equating our willingness to show mercy to His willingness to share mercy with us. Mercy is an expression of compassion that, once received, is to be shared with others.

We have received God's grace and mercy as unworthy as we were. Yet, that same grace and mercy now count us as worthy, not on our own, but through the gift of God. By the work of the Holy Spirit within us, that gift is intended to be extended to others just as unworthy as we once were.

If grace and mercy live in us, it will not be a struggle to pass it on. That, after all, is the nature of both.

About the Author

Pastor Tekisha D. Wimbush is a Native of Cleveland, Ohio. She is a minister of the Gospel of Jesus Christ and the wife of Bishop Willie J. Wimbush Jr., Church of the Reform Church of Love in Cleveland, Ohio.

Lady Wimbush's commitment to serving and helping others is evident through her lifestyle of service and dedication to the families and communities she serves. She diligently works with the Women's Ministry at Church of the Reform Church of Love to promote unity and sisterhood. She frequently hosts prayer and Women's Forum meetings, retreats, workshops, and other events to empower women to develop and grow in the love of God. In addition, Lady Wimbush serves in various ministries within The Church of the Reform, including Adult Sunday School Teacher, Church Finance/Administration Committee, Praise Team, Engagement / Program Coordinator, Youth Ministry, and Outreach.

Lady Wimbush has a 15-year history of employment with a Social Service agency in Cleveland, Ohio, where she supervised for over seven years. Lady Wimbush currently serves as a Licensed Social Worker for a Cleveland Hospice Agency, providing supportive comfort care. She also provides Clinical Counseling at a Cleveland Counseling Agency.

She holds multiple Master's Degrees in Social Work and Early Childhood Education and a Bachelor's Degree in Business Administration and Social Science. Lady Wimbush has a heart that resonates with restoring family relationships in a holistic modality. Lady Wimbush engages with both Macro and Micro community outreach to coordinate services to support those in need.

With all her accomplishments, she still considers supporting her husband in ministry and raising God-fearing children her primary purpose. As a mother of three, now adult, children, she firmly affirms that the best way to raise successful children is to be an active role model in demonstrating the love and fear of the Lord, which is the beginning of Wisdom.

TekishaDWimbush.com

facebook.com/TekishaDWimbush

instagram.com/tekishadwimbush

www.ingramcontent.com/pod-product-compliance
Lightning Source LLC
Chambersburg PA
CBHW072021110526
44592CB00012B/1398